HOW TO MAKE AN ALGORITHM IN THE MICROWAVE

ETEL ADNAN POETRY SERIES

Edited by
Hayan Charara and Fady Joudah

HOW TO MAKE
AN ALGORITHM
IN THE MICROWAVE

Maya Salameh

The University of Arkansas Press
Fayetteville : 2022

ISBN: 978-1-68226-213-9
eISBN: 978-1-61075-782-9

26 25 24 23 22   5 4 3 2 1

Manufactured in the United States of America

Designed by Liz Lester

∞ The paper used in this publication meets the minimum requirements of the American
National Standard for Permanence of Paper for Printed Library Materials Z39.48-1984.

Library of Congress Cataloging-in-Publication Data

Names: Salameh, Maya, author.
Title: How to make an algorithm in the microwave / Maya Salameh.
Description: Fayetteville: The University of Arkansas Press, 2022. | Series: Etel Adnan
   poetry series | Summary: "In How to Make an Algorithm in the Microwave, winner of
   the 2022 Etel Adnan Poetry Prize, Maya Salameh explores the intimate relationships
   we have with our devices, speaking back to the algorithm that serves simultaneously
   as warden, data thief, and confidant"—Provided by publisher.
Identifiers: LCCN 2022006846 (print) | LCCN 2022006847 (ebook) |
   ISBN 9781682262139 (paperback; alk. paper) | ISBN 9781610757829 (ebook)
Subjects: LCGFT: Poetry.
Classification: LCC PS3619.A425556 H69 2022 (print) | LCC PS3619.A425556
   (ebook) | DDC 811/.6—dc23/eng/20220218
LC record available at https://lccn.loc.gov/2022006846
LC ebook record available at https://lccn.loc.gov/2022006847

Supported in part by the King Fahd Center for Middle East Studies
at the University of Arkansas.

```html
<p>Choose your monster's features:</p>

<div>
<input type="checkbox" id="scales" name="scales"
checked>
<label for="torso">Scales</label>
</div>


<div>
<input type="checkbox" id="scales" name="mouth"
checked>
<label for="Mouth">Scales</label>
</div>


<div>
<input type="checkbox" id="scales" name="torso">
<label for="ribs">mouth</label>
</div>
```

CONTENTS

ALPHABET

ANAPHORA

FOREWORD

Maya Salameh's writing unravels the coding of language, strings its functions like fairy lights across cities on different continents. Folded multilingually like the baffling instructions that accompany electronic equipment, Salameh's poems school us on intergenerational relationships, eros, and the transglobal body in our barb-wired world. Experimental, exciting, playful, "her accent hasn't [been] invented yet."

Maya Salameh, your voice is in my clothes now. Teach me the algorithms of diaspora and write what the earth will look like in the decades after my death. Are we the color strokes Etel imagined in a San Francisco sunset painting of the future? Thank you for talking back at the computers, growing evergreen fronds across the motherboard. Thank you for observing the devices that are observing us, supposedly serving us. When we become cyborgs as the Anthropocene draws to its hot dusty end, I want your book next to me as translator. I want it now, to change the code. Thank you for your inimitable wryness:

> Arabic stands in my doorway / asks if there is space in my bed
> for her hands. /   / afterwards / I fold my tongue & get dressed

Plus, Homs really does sit uncomfortably with me at dinner; I excuse myself to smoke on the balcony to get away from her but that's when the bombs start barreling our neighborhood—how do you know these things so quirkily? Wainek, now I know it was you who ate up the cherries Syria was saving for me in the back of the refrigerator! بالهنا و الشفا because long may your translocated-Arab-feminist fingers muck up the machine. When you want, I want with you, "a train station where no one is taken from someone he loves," "a trolley car full of Fairouz & women & no one instructing"—and I want "my girlfriends' countries back."

You notice everywhere the gendered body and follow its curvature, chasing it even into the MRI cylinder, into the recesses of how grandmother's mind works with Alzheimer's. You mirror the intimacies of mothers and daughters getting dressed as time spools and the body's platelet count deteriorates. Your poem "might daughter itself into wheat" as you wordplay across English, French, Arabic, and Spanish, cartwheeling nouns into verbs, goddesses into stars semicoloned on your elbows. You make Punnett Square poems of our ancestry crossed with Amy Winehouse and a pack of cigarettes, but leave them open for potential. How can I quote a Punnett Square poem?

We need a new poetry lexicon—a new way of moleculing the poem on the page, even—and Maya Salameh brings it. We need all the strange Arabic-diasporic ways we can find for being in this terrible and joyful and often frighteningly banalizing world, and Salameh's poems are a generous find. Her writing is an unexpected cousin in the colonized and capitalism-razed city, bewildering and divining things you've never heard but want to learn now you've met them. Prepare to be stretched and delighted.

MOHJA KAHF

ANGEL / RECURSION

Neatness, reward, puns, delight in song, joy, illustrations, laughter, pictures, beauty, shapeliness, the beat of string instruments, loving one's bride, and seeking spices and things that smell good. She delivers dreams and provokes games of chess. She desires to sleep with women, to strengthen love with them, and she longs for faithfulness from them. She governs the desire to appear beautiful, to love freedom. She abhors quarrels, vengeance, and lawsuits. She welcomes false oaths and is inclined towards desire. She desires to drink excessively. She incessantly desires abundant sex in filthy ways and inappropriate places. She governs exerting fairness in things, being loved by women, being loved by men, being a host, involving oneself in the manufacture of crowns, making stable things, operating from stones, having a sweet skill, looking down on the world with no fear of it.

—Characterization of Venus, *Picatrix*

Since there was no way we could agree on the basis of reason, I resorted to irrationality. It was up to the white man to be more irrational than I. For the sake of the cause, I had adopted the process of regression, but the fact remained that it was an unfamiliar weapon; here I am at home; I am made of the irrational; I wade in the irrational. Irrational up to my neck.

—Frantz Fanon

Ambivalence regarding the degree to which one's appearance is visibly "Arabic," especially in regard to the darkness of skin color, may emerge in family therapy, particularly for children.

—*Ethnicity and Family Therapy*

APARTMENT: a body with stairs; noun: the faucets moon. the asbestos moans.

ALGORITHM: is a sacred object. it summarizes.

LOOP: not a very good daughter. she takes long walks to think about nothing, moths. nasty habit of refraction. met her in San Francisco on a book tour.

VENUS: the sister.

ALEPPO: the cousin.

ALGORITHM: threads pulled out of a computer. bits can be found in the veins. like no more watching.

BOOLEAN: numerology, i.e., a code & a homily are both instructions.

DAMASCUS: jasmine (apartment) (playground) (store)

ALGORITHM: a computer's admission to blood. this makes the screen just as fallible & possibly anemic.

MARS: visits occasionally, leaves his shoes on in my room.

SAN DIEGO: America's Finest City.

VENUS: see in the neighborhood of page 59. likes her eyeliner navy & underneath like it's 2006.

AMY: famed British pop singer. miracle with nicked ankles.

ALGORITHM: derived from the Latin noun *algorismus*, mangled transliteration of the Arabic name *al-Khwarizmi* (mathematician who introduced algebra to Europe).

LANGUAGE: the way an apartment finds a home in the throat.

DAMASCUS: rules over rain, fire, differences, burial, the lack of comforts, sharpness.

DAUGHTER: recursion.

TUTORING: a service required of English learners. service rendered as compensation for having so much dialect in the teeth.

TRANSLATION: the alphabet's revenge on the body.

THE IDEA OF THE VIRGIN MARY: shrine by my father's desk, left corner by the windows. mahogany wood & four effigies of the same blue-draped woman.

BOOLEAN: being able to count, e.g., I'm not *only* a woman.

FAIROUZ: renowned Lebanese singer. has recorded over 1,500 songs. claims she is singing as if praying.

RECURSION: daughter.

REDDING: to autumn, to blush. cedars & trucks.

BOOLEAN: girl, bed, neck.

SLEEP APNEA WITH CITY BLOCK

one night the street is to the left the next its artery is repaved. nine six one, my mother

watches me in the bathroom, the house shrinks to the fabric across my breasts &

haven't I been good? crossed my legs for the priests & capitalists? six one it takes me

four neighborhoods to fall asleep. I scrape the skin off nectarines. six one nine. the rich

devour my coast, buying homes by the same ocean that stole so many husbands. the

sea is the last wife & teenagers dump electronics in her lap. six one nine. it's the end

of January & I'm still anemic.[1] nine six I pull her shirt & make myself an altar.

six one a street is built like this: an icon sold a limb of cement, a relic found the

Internet, I stashed the orange moon under my fifth molar & it's been feeding me ever

since. nine six one & Lemon Grove looks like the Mediterranean from two blocks down

& once I dreamt I had a daughter. I never slept again. six one Saida, like cicadas in

August. six one I am singing. it is the rosary again. I want to be ordinary,

intact as a man in uniform. nine six I sing like an elegy with a city in it.

---

1 *The War on Terror was not defined by a geography, a time bracket, or an established rubric for its targets. The ambiguity of the target was not an oversight by the U.S. intelligence regime but rather a deliberate political strategy that demonstrates the way racial ambiguity works in service to racialized violence and exclusion [. . .] ambiguity of the target is a necessary and intentional characteristic.* (Censusless, Loubna Qutami)

the first summer I spent away from home I decided I loved a boy who was just getting into religion & litanied about women being queens this was before I started therapy & realized how much of that was a euphemism for work I ate a lot of salads but only if there were cherry tomatoes in them

BLOOD WORK

my brother eats only Apple
Jacks for breakfast unless
mama made the pancakes with
extra eggs he hands me
the apparel of his silence
a video game a book about dolphins
he adores purple Fanta & one night my brother
chased a veridian melon down the street it
felt like a bad analogy for the length
of his name we watch Men in Black
it is July his country for sale
in coffee shops he asks me if I'd like ginger
ale or apple juice I search my tooth fillings
for diamonds I forge the sun's signature on
her visa papers Beirut him in the back of the head
he writes *hacer hacer hacer* in its six iterations
asks where do I put my marrow
they make professions from this
we lie under his navy blanket
count the earrings underneath his pillow
like small insurrections & he smiles
like he doesn't know how much hemoglobin
costs the long sorrow of the color red
I know what happens to boys

MEMORY IS A SOFTWARE

func(fraction)	*your grandmother is a quarter Armenian & your father once denied he was from Trablos. we are not really "Arab." who is really "from"*
func(weight)	I was always a skinny girl ÷ we fry yolks on pavement
func(loop)	desire is an old family heirloom none of the women in my family approximately jacarandas on my dress
func(autopsy)	my mother in her emerald swimsuit
func(anaphora)	clothes are about waiting growing into the jacket coat sweats
func(Thomas)	jiddo the numismatist & me quarter the girl I should be ÷ I make odalisques in the mirror cover my face in yolk
func(fraction)	I am an approximation of jacarandas
func()	clothes are about waiting my baptism name is Mariam
func(sacrament)	the priest wrings the solar system from my mouth

CVS ALTERCATION ft. AMY WINEHOUSE

I read once a woman had her baby taken away because she ate   a bagel with poppy

seeds   in it. Amy drives above the speed limit   & she is iridescent & wide-eyed. the

rim of her voice bends when she speaks to men   I notice how she excises the

honey from her throat. we stop   to buy a frozen pizza for the stove in our house that

spills from the seams.   we develop like

gasoline in aisle seven. Freud strolls by the detergents & *jinsik*? & my gender is manna

found in an unmarked van. I read once a woman had her baby taken

because she ate a wafer with an incision in it.   Amy says in heaven it is always

autumn. we   marinate tires in wine for the best taste. *jinsik*? Amy & I leave

smuggling sleeves of Junior Mints & she sings   like enough blood.

CADILLAC ALGORITHM

1. the archive retches & the bride is hair
   stockpiled in ringlets, peonies on the couch. she is still
   24 & she smiles like Aleppo with her makeup off.
   a man is like a business: a man is an
   endeavor: a man is a Euphrates you make
   to your children.

2. the bride is young in a country
   her accent hasn't invented yet, & she is gorgeous. the
   daughter is wrinkled with the cassettes she played past 30. but
   the bride has no daughters yet & you can tell she has slept. the bride
   thus becomes archival process, smiling like she's eaten her three eggs
   in the morning. the calendar winks. the color of her dress is yolk.

2.5. (I tell her I'm on the last day of my cycle. I volunteer news
   of my abdomen. she's a notary but mostly a recovering
   mathematician, new numbers to rectify the old measurements. once
   stripped of certainty, an engineer is only a prophet. she
   scratches at her email. our body, contested/accounted on a screen.)

3. June & I make the bride drive
   me to unit 180, pour 60 negatives on the tile. I can't find command
   hooks for the stills but the store-bought elegy works fine. you
   wash your feet in the tub, I'm a 99cent Magdalene in the frame
   of the door with no hinges, & this too
   is an archival process: you with your hair down,

filling the hallway with lace, ensuring I have a neck
to inherit for the ceremony.

3.3. you atone your hair above the sink,
we let the pictures rot in our desks. we floss. we forget. I open
the frame. out spills your long striped dress, your friend's peach
Cadillac, your canines still intact.

2

2 *The Arabic word for sex,* jins, *appeared sometime in the early twentieth century carrying with it not only its old meanings of type and kind and ethnolinguistic origin, but also new meanings of biological sex and nationality. The word in the sense of type and kind has existed in Arabic since time immemorial and is derived from the Greek genus. As late as 1870, its connotation of sex had not yet come into usage. An unspecific word for sexuality,* jinsiyyah—*which also means nationality and citizenship—was coined in the 1950s by translators of the works of Freud.* (Re-Orienting Desire, Joseph Massad)

GHOSTS COME FREE ON FEAST DAYS

take the bundle of chestnuts

only three dollars. feel
this sweater. like sowing your skin back

together after a swim. taste
this mansaf. like the voice of a woman

who hasn't lost her eyes yet.

come. there's
a dress in the back

waiting to try you on.

PUNNETT SQUARE

	A	A
A	my sister my liver my sister smiling & endless my sister ringed with silver & all the spleen she still has my sister splinters	
a		my river blisters

HOW TO FIX AN ELEVATOR IN TRABULSI

the mice

in the
elevator
apologize

about the
hole in the
sixth floor

often
reserved for
weddings my
breasts

bleed black
milk I was
mostly a
mother on

days I wasn't
the mice
insist against
the buttons

so I gorge
flights of gray
stairs

slacks
creased with
sleep

WHEN HAIL APPEARS IF A MENSTRUATING WOMAN THROWS HERSELF ONTO THE GROUND COMPLETELY NAKED RAISING HER LEGS TOWARD THE CLOUD THE HAIL WILL NOT FALL AROUND HER ON THAT FIELD OR HARVEST (LAYOVER IN SEATTLE)

so I'm walking to gate 24 trying to get to my flight because Massachusetts won't last forever. I'm on my period trying to keep from desecrating my leggings & my boots have red soles & it's raining. not pearling or flaking, raining. everywhere mothers are slipping beanies on sons. I'm listening to my aching playlist, this lady stops me by the Panda Express to ask me the time & it's Fairouz. my temples are splitting mom thinks birth control will shrink my eggs my headphones spill. I text Nina hey are you still waiting for clots? did roomie buy you the Fireball? Fairouz gesticulates with her larynx, unbuckles her belt. would Amy be stopped in an airport? they are both eyelined & blackhaired, Fairouz with her voice full of crows. I'm seeping & the pretzels are sweet & if hail appears my language might daughter itself into wheat.

CALCULUS FOR ANEMICS

the apartment moves like fire going blind. the floor bends   spine of old book.
Sometimes my attention eclipses   static dipped in milk. my cortex
hums & she walks symmetrically,   holy books.   most days
my type is bored & built but my third eye's starting to open   or I'm too invested in the
idea of searing,   tasting a night from seventeen again in case it burns better this
time. I'm a romantic   obsess about her hands while I ignore the seminar
about emotional   intelligence my scholarship thinks will cure the recession. &
there's a recession   in my gums I haven't told anyone about, not even the
angels, & I talk disconnected, like a botched baptism. Sometimes my attention eclipses

according to Corinthians, I microwave oatmeal, listen > to birds, fill the bin with unsuccessful chains of psalms. // the apostle sits at his desk & tries rendering the verse: a boy, saffron permeating the room. what experience did I have
of asking.

> we sit in the grass, repeating our abbreviated stories. here is my
pistachio house on Campanile Drive. here is my front porch.

["kiss","graduate","contents","pecan","suffocate","sweetheart","laughter","knitting","volcano", "broom","vanilla","paradise","curtains","oven","hammer","hosanna","slaughter","coyote", "hairdryer","promotion","hyacinth","seasick","cash","hunter","miracle","fingerprint","milk", "duct","romantic","funeral","freezer","palm"]

< but some evenings my desk will // widen & I will be young & unknown, sitting in my wicker chair committing new praises, the sunlight like a river of milk. a sermon >> is politics. I think of his shoulders, wide
as parabolas. // I
fondle my binary through my shirt. we call this > Leviathans.

ELEGY WITH AMY

the doctors don't know what to do with me / maybe I'm out of
platelets / maybe I've been watched too much / my grandmother was a
lavender comb & lemonfaced / when the doctor asked for a health history I
told him my uncles were sixty percent smoke / my hair in helixes / the
nursing home in May & it's over 80 the flowers are reeking / she is
bedridden & the MRI beeps next to MTV / the crooners propagate her
months / Amy / our women live to ninety / summer & my headphones
your starving / you sing / Amy / the country we're all subletting is dying /
they still sell Monsters on Euclid / Amy / my grandmother sang Halim until
she forgot him / her voice is in my clothes & yours //// I think of her
nineteen in front of a blackboard numbers splayed across her ribs / the
doctor's estimations / four months three ventilators / we sit in the TV room
with another episode of The Beautiful & The Bold / the nurse pulls the
wide yellow curtain behind us like a mandated sun & isn't that beauty /
being told / Amy they promised me iron pills & neurologists & grief tastes
different in Arabic / kinda pistachio / after the funeral / me & her son sit in
a plastic booth & my camisole can't fit my thorax / // Amy / you both spoke
like a pack of Newports // all I wanted was to keep her from dying in
French / the swivel table & word salad / Amy / I dreamed the buildings
finally spilled from your throat / that all the omitted women fell from the
songs & no one forgot them / last month I lost her turquoise bracelet /
hoping she'd call & scold me / her voice would comb over my scalp again /
exponentiate & pull

WILL KITTY GENOVESE EVER STOP DYING

in the textbook there are either thirty-eight
faces or forty-nine, an alley of brick.
they diffuse their eyes from terror
like molasses. I lather my body,

the discourse, with pear blossom soap.
I scrape continent from under my fingernails,
smear my orange hunger on the windshield. it
is powerful to be witnessed.

LARYNX

I think a lot about the fact
I've never fucked with my hands.

I've tweezed & nicked
at nearly everything else. but I watch

my cuticles chip, indexes wide
as reproach. mama loved men

with all the fervor of God. instead I wait
for a sage bra to arrive in the mail, allow

a boy's big hands unrequiting my hips. her
in a blank moment by her desktop,

clipping her nails with scissors. the Hudson
is a two hour walk. the thing above my bed

is forgetting. like a grammarian, I pick at the
idioms pinking my cheeks, & my hair is long

& venerable,   aged as waiting
for scripture to expire. she hits forks against

the intestines of the sink. she husks pomelos
in the driveway. I want to be maintained on a

table, remembered at my starchest & most
angry, shrined against a wall,

vilified well.
amen.

54 LINE (DEBUGGED)

we meet in parking lots the developers
call useless. the screens blink
to rectify the price of bread.

DATA THE ALGORITHM KNOWS ABOUT MEN

they trained the officer in Jerusalem. (both men
spoke of holy lands
with cartridges in their gums, or God

is the taste of grass.) a gobstopper: spit, America,
blood. my father
once fell through a roof. your sons
are almost men. they raze the duplex

like teeth to bone. they're building the bloom
the doctors want.

ALPHABET

Je fais du nomadisme comme d'autres accomplissent leur périple quotidien entre leur domicile et leur lieu de travail.

L'arabe: ma maison. Le français: mon lieu de travail.

L'arbre pour moi est plus arbre, plus feuillu quand il s'appelle Chajarat. La tristesse est plus intense quand elle s'appelle Hozn. La mer plus vaste quand elle s'appelle Bahr. J'essaie de trouver le mot le plus près de la chose, celui qui reflète mieux qu'un autre mon enfance dans mon village, pour y retrouver la puissance des femmes près du feu, l'eau, les herbes qu'elles accommodaient comme je le fais des mots arabes et français mélangés à quantité égale pour une nourriture écrite.

—Vénus Khoury-Ghata

English will have to phone
and leave message after message of desire on our machines
English will have to learn what to say to please us

—Mohja Kahf

THESAURUS ENTRY

the ridges underneath the dining table are
green, like being twenty five & new, an apartment
on Baltimore Drive, the emaciated kitchen with emerald tupperware
& a daughter is a reason. green like cucumber cream cheese sandwiches or
how to ululate. a daughter
is precious for the duration of her keeping; noun: daughter is precious for watching. a
daughter is precious for smiling while watched, gutting the television with her eyes.
green like the difference between the words venerate & confess, lamb hearts on a
plastic table, a verdant Tuesday in July & driving all the way to Aleppo without
stopping. green an apartment on Baltimore Drive, the mossy drywall chipping,
a migraine straddling a daughter who like the drywall is chipping. noun:
ululation: a daughter is precious for watching, for spare drywall. green.
they said in the mall at Oceanside girls were coaxed into vans by
ladies who called themselves Mothers of God. green mom &
her Braun, nicked with omissions. I grew up watching her
flinch. I inherited that movement. green Coltrane on the
radio, saline drips, if I cut out the part of me that wants
will my hair grow back less thick. outside the
apartment there's the stump of a willow tree,
marriage of hazel & mud, I'm embarrassed
by the miracle I'm becoming.
Zoey's house with the teal porch, a foulbreathed eulogy on the
grass, amber streetlights & swings & the apartment haunted
by billboards. green a daughter under a balcony in a
discounted coat. ululation: green an orchard in the
cornea the doctor calls astigmatism. green an
apartment on Baltimore Drive & the graves
under the cement ululate & a daughter
is precious for watching. green
the well-loved playground
our bus can reach &
green wishing to
fluent something.
that green.

I FIND ANTONIO BANDERAS BORING

every day I can't stand my reflection is also an accomplishment, a testament to your terrible joy or how you refuse to dye your roots back to black. tomorrow is your forty sixth birthday & this feels symmetrical, me twenty sleeping in the garage & you being mistaken for decades. your favorite trench is the color of roadkill. the prescription on your lenses should be renewed but we joke about the wait in front of the Chuze gym instead. we drive to Costco & dream of all the chemicals we haven't bought, mascara, ginger, ammonia. the dentist says my back left molar should be watched. we listen to Banderas again & you say he'd really be able to count someone limb by limb. you are still reading the same sixth grade Spanish grammar textbook & you hack conjugations with the delicacy of marigolds. men love singing about women with all their hair but recoil from the nearest thing with teeth. you just got your notary license & one Wednesday this month you called me a miracle while splitting tomatoes. when you were my age your favorite Jackson track was thriller, the red jacket & the granite he made of your cramped apartment. your striated back, like a rifle wilting. we're laughing by the fridge & I decree a new collection, sixty songs that sound like a mountain kneeling. I tell you god has had enough paintings written about him. later we fight about how many children I'll have & my throat starts rivering again. I hide in my room. I'm listening to Bryson like he wrote it for me, & I'm trying on all my earrings. the day closes like a platelet & I floss around my canines while you sing with your bra off. somewhere under my epidermis is a beautiful woman sleeping. I keep scrubbing & scrubbing until she comes out.

CLEANING ORBEEZ OUT OF THE YARD IN DECEMBER

we kneel to the cement, pick jade
spheres from the ground. yesterday we lobbed
pink at each other laughing because we knew
they'd evaporate & the sun did our work for us
but it rained last night & today
the yard covered in pastel. you snitched but
make the dino nuggets we like as apology. now
two siblings brooming through afternoon,
tossing gems in the neighbor's pool.

FAIROUZ & AMY DEBATE OVER DESSERT

which river are you from?

> the colder one. you?

I'm
the moon's neighbor.

> I stole
> a radio to eat.

one must be allowed
to grieve alone.

> I escaped from the roof. I took my
> incisors, my unfair salary,
> all my allotted blood.

you stole my earrings.

> you sing a lot of songs
> about beautiful girls. why not
> change the words.

why translate women?

you sing like carotid.

5:38PM

I'm alive.

> you're
> waking the neighbors.

> lunch?

I invited the Euphrates. I hope
you don't mind.

I measure my desire in radials. I'm
I measure my desire in radials. I'm
the voice of the morning.
the voice of the morning.

NATIVE SPEAKER

Arabic at the dinner table / spearing mint / Spanish leaves her soiled hymns

in the laundry / tries teaching French how to ululate / I laugh at them

both / Arabic stands in my doorway / asks if there is space in my bed

for her hands /   / afterwards / I fold my tongue & get dressed

noon

& you

were the noun

that slicked my pages

with sweat. you astride

the elliptical‹ like the stretch

of the letter ن. noon. noun. nu:un. I marry

my thumb to your mouth. ن. you swallow caffeine pills‹ pin

me with purple irises. your blue-tinted body. what a relief to be a terrified woman. I

write the noon 40 times. the sun scribes me onto stone tablets. ن & you

were the noun that slicked my pages with sweat.

SONATA WITH ALZHEIMER'S

my
grandmother
the
schoolteacher is
forgetting
comments on
the facebook
post flagged for
my family name
types her village
(runny vowels)
(crucifix ironed
on wrist) we
deface our
smartmouthed
phones with our
loud prayers &
pillshaped nails

my grandmother versus explaining fig
trees fresh linen her beekeeper neighbor
she gestures empty to the screen
paints the word with her arm
one day she will have ink poisoning

a student of hers namesaked his first
daughter after her (Rosa) ((my mother's
wilting recall) (my migraines)) she smears
the alphabet on a wall

her family was
full of farmers
some butchers
over breakfast
she reads tea
leaves
looking for
nuptials or
wraiths (my
grandfather
languages his
wife) (my
mother says
this is good for
her memory)

we dial the number in PST & she beams
at her daughter who mirrors her (this
forgetting which mangles our women)
girls with my body sojourn the same
Damascus (radiator yolk alley) they visit
& vigil & visit until the city flattens

RIVER ALGORITHM

THE PACIFIC CAN ONLY CALL ME AFTER EIGHT * THE RED WEARS ONLY

BROWN DRESSES * BREAKS ARTICHOKE HEARTS OFF MY PLATE * I AM

SERENADING THE EUPHRATES TO SLEEP * I AM SINGING TO HER STILL

lean in to please the ghost in me & I'll bloom, calm from being held down. your arms bunch at the ends. like honeycomb. you remind me of all the dirt & good liver left & pronounce my name while altaring me through a screen. you make a river in the algorithm, midnight smears the roof. we kiss like there are words for it in Arabic. sixty degrees on Halloween & I'll tape last minute nouns to my breasts. I'll clean you off my teeth.

---

3 *A cyborg woman touches herself for three reasons:*

    1. to inspect the machinery for errors;
    2. to convince herself she is a mammal;
    3. to pull herself apart.

                (*Soft Science,* Franny Choi)

IN PARIS,
YOUNES BENDJIMA CARRIES THE PRESIDENT & PROPOSES TO GRANDMA

we're at a basketball game which is
wrong because Bendjima is a boxer & Macron
has torn his ACL so he lays on
the Algerian's back. the 6-footer bends, asking
for Esperanza's hand. I am sitting on her knee &
she blushes. I dance her towards cracks
in the pavement, thousands of dollars
worth of organs on the sidewalk. she said often
that revolution was a braid. I arrange guava taffy
on my desk in order of each *ente 3omri*. you are my
lifespan. the linoleum echoes. she is picking
at my dandruff, gossiping over rice.

OPEN WINDOW AT 3PM

the sun traipses through the panes: all these
postcolonial classes & I still think I am ugly

Hail Mary	Folding Instructions
sixteen sitting in the back of a red Camry trying not to let rosary spill from my mouth.	
I was named after water & my want is a well-built desk, curved	like the sound of the law
scraping itself against the windshield. suffused	
(Mary sitting in a manger or a laundromat, tapping an invisible music out on her laptop, the congregation in print. intrinsic as language, or phonetics, fumbling next to someone in the dark.)	
	with waiting , I re word the litany tinting my spine, & the hand on the altar is provisional & a bit cold, heavy with
novenas. girl	with her appetites all open. I swallow the statistic of my length, my willful, lanky body. I aspire to be recited, spilled
	on a keyboard, now & at the hour . bism al salib.

MORPHEME BUILDING

morpheme > building > mama > civil engineer with mosaic disk >

meridian: rehearses grocery bill (refuses epidural)

meridian: slick music of mottled stomach

morpheme: fluently speaks of other men

specialty: water sanitation > if: this body is a girl:

meridian stomach > > a building

is just > a prayer with walls: (marriage a mural)

chipping off the sink > mama > rogue

engineer: with the mosaic stomach > feeds

my father grapes > as he drives > > drapes

like the Atlantic

ALGORITHM WITH PANTS UNBUTTONED (SHAHWAH)

I split the fridge's innards for carrot cake think about 4:45pm the reek of gasoline * he

looks at me like the dent in our Corolla * Christopher Columbus has been decapitated in

Boston * the summer is new & stubborn * he can buy his sisters branded backpacks with

the Adobe check * I can only promise mine diagnoses * I try leaning

in the booth like girls who've inherited apartments in soho * men in jerseys are

jackaling themselves on the TV * on Twitter three war criminals take cool pictures

together * my brother keeps asking for Roblox gift cards * the screen opens &

swallows the walls * I cobble together the pen amputated under my mattress let the

wax pool like a clot * I am running out of diaphragm * this at least feels consensual * I

tuck my spoon into frosting * think about clouds * wine * flirt like the next sixty days

won't be an anaphora in my throat when I am drunk * afterwards we keep messaging

needing to prove our teeth * I amend calligraphy in him with my nails the highway is

littered with green stalks * such gorgeous words but none he can eat

the sun
is a rude cousin with no empathy.
aria aber

what would love do
if I died.
adonis

RECURSION (STOMACH)

func(stomach)	my mother was begotten	by a tired woman
func(womb)	she presses her palm to my stomach	this makes a meridian
func(dialect)	together we miscarry a language	in this way we share a son
func(womb)	Naima	(Coltrane & she inherited the clots from her mother
func(stomach)	the horn determined	an ovary) I clean
func(womb)	the dining table with bleach	the horn slivered & serene slow as the tired body
func(dialect)	she presses her palm to my stomach	
func(daughter)		wants my double or hers
func(dialect)	middle class altered gait night terrors	the psalms here
func(womb)	kiss	the cervix
func(stomach)		one day I will have a daughter

_____

4 A government soldier in Salma (a village of the Latakia province) following its recapture from rebels, January 15, 2016.

recursion {emulsion, gears, teeth}
recursion {*bint*}
recursion {I was a boy growing up}

new algorithm_with crinkles around it that demonstrate_the age to
which I survived: I'm still

lipsticked somewhere_inebriating the room. there's
Venus remnants_ in my ears

& my throat is full. I
gesture like the Colorado_I am old enough to be conscripted.

bint: between my ribs it smells

like cigarettes & cracked oranges. \ recursion (there's \

no difference between musicians & women.) \

I am one fifty three pounds [five foot eight]. *bint*: I am a growing

[boy who forgets to eat]. I'm wearing my
getcatcalledjeans, cracked
algorithm. Europa,

Io, Metis: my gender, Callisto:
recursion: teeth,
emulsion, girlgearsmoon.

girl: the sound raah,

a fine auntie who's lived the definition saying mashallah. like watching a man with
your uncle's name tease a woman named Yasmeen or

*<p> during WWI, a British and French blockade (1915-18) of the Syrian
coastline impeded the entry of food and caused the deaths (from starvation) of more than
100,000 people (a quarter of the population) </p>*

analysts lining up and one by one tracing
my lips. girl: *bint*: I array
my testament body like all I ask is

a witness &
maybe my eyes / riddled with the inherited potential
for cataracts / I clatter through

the artery of the road / do we inherit hungers? / Mercury a
geometrician, shuffling back
into jeans. I grew up

making saints out of men.

AMY TELLS THE OFFICER WHAT HAPPENED

the moschino bra you bought me
last christmas

river
of no return:

we were alone
your rolled up sleeves

you know
I'm no good

the moschino bra
your neighbors

I'll be some next man's
other woman soon

47

the next boy was a computer science major & vented about how hard it was to buy condoms how much he loved his sisters the lights above his bed were red & pulsed in the corners of the room like pinned hummingbirds & he was skinny but packing & kinda fine in his glasses I ate a lot of lucky charms that week mostly for the marshmallows cause my period was driving me crazy & I was starting to think that luck & vitamins were bullshit

QUERY EXERCISES // ALGORITHM WITH CHERRIES

for Mohja Kahf

1. Homs sets the table, asks about your ceasefires & unhappy sisters, but she can never sit comfortably with you at dinner. you watch her fix her fuchsia lipstick / adjust the cocktail dress that fits her like a mermaid.

2. speaking of the sea, Latakia is dressed in her swimsuit & eager to leave the house before her parents spot her empty shoulders. there are polka dots / this time they are not exit wounds.

3. as usual Aleppo is asking after you in an empty restaurant. she is wearing your jersey. she does not particularly like soccer but she watches the Ionic column of your calves as you play / she croons the road.

4. Homs will never admit it, but she is saving a bowl of cherries in the back of the refrigerator for you / she is still waiting for the day the secret police stop returning her metaphors with twisted elbows.

5. Damascus cuts her hair short as her temper, sneaks a cigarette on the balcony / bleeds a little when she dances.

A TINY NOW TO FEED ON

auntie smiles symmetrically, hoists
my sister on her shoulders. she's coming
back from the anniversary party of a

marriage we later learn is polyester. for
now all her cuspids align * three uncles
debate my birth time in the basement of

the apartment building with gray tubs.
I am eight, framed by roofs, grates,
the pink cake I didn't prefer to

chocolate * mama beams with me
on her hip, a cathedral in a dress. her
earrings are small & cling to her neck

like a metaphor about the ocean * at dinner
she & all her sisters rise from the table
& start undulating. I watch them dance

pupils wide as moon * grandma with
the gray eyes, threatening the camera
* my sister & I sleep calm as pavement,

the sleeves of her sweater crowd her wrists. I
milk the stars for blood. I am in a coral shirt
with daisy trimming *

HOW TO LAZARUS YOURSELF

Santa Monica & your uncle in an empty house, singing like the interstate. palms pressed to the pews of the Syriac Catholic Church's fundraised hall & you see? the saints never leave us, even when we can't afford to live in actual Los Angeles.

commiserate about the cost of homes in Chula Vista. find a soccer player to fill time with. a boy is an accessory to a story, tasteless & overpriced. romanticize absence, chemicals, playing a song you love for friends & realizing the hook is lazy.

pass dramatically & selfishly, the way women aren't entitled to motorcycle accidents.

don't make an amenable saint.

when the time comes you intend to die with your limbs unsalvageable & yours, somewhere you don't have any cousins. maybe Seattle.

learn to fill a room like Esperanza, inhaling the citrus out the walls & blooming. kill the constitutions under your bed & survive with an open window & arteries that still function. afterwards your poems are gory but you are still around to write them.

watch your sun in the mirror. call your mother & talk about traffic or the cost of apples. don't mention the insomnia or her portrait of the Son bleeding out.

AT THE END OF JULY WE SAW A BROWN BEAR FROM 10 FEET AWAY & I ASKED ABOUT WHAT ATTRACTS MAMMALS TO THE FOREST & ALICIA SAID THE SMELL OF EVERYTHING EVEN LOTION

everything in the bed is washed the navy comforter the synthetic silk pillowcases & the

night before I'd gone into the forest (without realizing my period was going to come the

next day in a perfect oval when I had just got done organizing the bathroom it was timed

elegantly & irregular for its beauty red & viscous & hungry like I'd been once before I'd

ever loved anybody) the night before my friends dragged me camping & it was Tahoe

& dark but I was laid in a thermal sleeping bag feeling a dam between my legs & for a

moment I felt like the Mariam I'd been named brows smeared with the effort of crossing

my ankles but even though no one would come with me outside I ventured a couple feet

from our yellow tent & squatted in the dirt for 4 minutes I swear the Jordan left me my

friend laughed from inside she said I was prolific & I was

PUNNETT WITH AMY

	A	A
A	like dime store gold, I pile on a couch for the holiday & shine like rust. I am six, the television is blaring. her hair a beehive, crosses piled on her neck. she scats her indigo stomach, Marlboros, staccato body, battered jeans.	algorhythm: Amy makes a pattern with her throat. the screen stutters. music is a technology: I serenade the headline from my marrow. her voice iridescent / my Arabic like me bent & arching / us on the kitchen floor, reciting my stomach.
a	Amy opens her mouth with a country in it, croons my ribs open. *fhemt*? my dress blossoms loudly & it is Boston. *bint* her testament, my tattered breasts. *fhemt*? words are a business. we bleed glottal for the audience. we confess elegant, without confessing.	there is the photo of her in an insincere smile. dad liked to say we were descended from royalty. he was lying but I walked like I believed him. the screen cracks. we pour in jasmine rain oranges. we peer back. I have a brittle conviction I will make a beautiful woman.

GOD IS AN IRON YOU CHOOSE

mom straightens her hair over a chair razes the texture from her head my mother loves

dead ends so I leave mine alone a queer twisted thing in the mirror I watch it coil I kiss

our deviated noses mama legs riddled with punctuation marks I slip platelets in her food

I've stolen many things but never my septum back

SCENES FROM A MARRIAGE

{

}

APOSTLE PAUL ASKS YOU FOR A ROOM

it's easy to be pretty for a day. but try keeping the pretty on
for a week. does the sixty include a second towel? a man
left his pulpit on my back. the night

is not so mean. it allows the glamours
of the dead. & there is time finally for books, enough
to fill every pyre to fullness, satiety even. not to fill

the gap, mind you. just to remedy the
dirt. did you say fifty? find me a boy
and I'll make him an empire. I'll wipe the

prophets off him, remind him he's a man. I'll
be staying a couple days. let's say
forty.

they leaked August's nudes on CNN today. there is the picture of my father in a flared

shirt I imagine is red because he was young & still getting used to wearing clothes

important enough to be stained. every Thanksgiving for six years in a row we roadtrip

to Vegas to inhale barbeque ribs & ogle the Bellagio. I am a jigsaw the physician puzzles

over for weeks. I have a growth on my back the shape of the apartment in Achrafieh & I

read Hemingway and Bukowski, all the drunks. I am of proper age. my sister is a semester

deep. they lost August's knees & on CNN my father watches his country's women abscess

the tv. at church they pass a basket for the dying. the incense cuts a meridian across my

larynx. I clean spouts the same way he does, with the back of my hands like the faucet is

atrophied. his neighborhood had a name once. I think I share this name somewhere in

my body, maybe the mole under my arm shaped like a watermelon seed or Tyre on her

knees. he laughs at the anesthesiologist, offers his veins. 17,000 disappeared when he left.

we must name these bodies. August & a used Buick & I've always thought martyrs were

the most handsome. I ask the cashier the cost of yams. I call the shards in my mouth oral

fixations. do you understand? myrrh is a very good coagulant.

---

5 *the eucalyptus are in bloom. the Arabs are under the ground. the Americans on the moon.* (Etel Adnan)

THE PRAYER OF THE BODY IS ATTENTION

I am the living proof green
melon apricots skin luminous
with fever no tragedies today I admire
the span of my ass in the mirror conjure
melancholy from me with daisy clips
here are both my breasts & my legs
I don't trust my body preceded me
by six centuries at least I am the living
proof incense blooming my sternum

ALGORITHM WITH BLUE EYELINER

1 Venus has a mouth

2 　　too big_for her god (once my mother

3 　　named sparrows) her favorite strain of red

5 the abacus in the laptop calls itself jinn

6 　　　# if (I overuse commas) else (add roots to dots)

8 I count (my veins) (my nicked algorithm) in the mirror

9 　　　　Venus feeds me an acronym　*　in a crowded restaurant

10

11 it's April_an archive is overall a lived process_a body_a moon

12 　　　# if (Venus was always going into stranger's cars) else (heel)

14 # an algorithm is a sacred object　　　　# it summarizes

16 　　　ie < Venus wears only magenta barrettes

17 　　　ie < Venus steals mousse from the CVS on Mission

19 　　　ie < my mother speaks slow&rivered_like ministering

20 　　　# I peel mangoes

21 　　　# I algorithm my throat

23 Venus an archive _ overall a

24 　　　　　relic in Wranglers _ looking for the door

26 how do you make an anaphora::?

27 　　girl # grammar # blood

THIS COUNTRY SMELLS OF NOT ENOUGH DOCTORS' OFFICES

so I sit in my room, do useless things. - I wait for the demise of the state, rewatch

Vampire Diaries, order pancakes riddled with blueberries. the officers switch lines in

front of us, badges glinting like chrysalis. if -- given the chance I'd ruin a man like a

monument, use my acrylics to mottle history into him. I drink tangerine

juice, put on the windows, stars, a cluster of empty parks. - I retch

America into the sink. I wear silk. -- my uncle works in a hospital. - the neighbors

disfigure a top 40 song next door & men who look like mine watch other men like the

officer does. thus the officer is replicated in the liquor store & the law - preserves

itself in aisle seven next to cherries in a jar. - - - a country is desires, appetite, ears,

hands, mouth. - the hospital I was born in

was called Zion. - the doctors - never warn you about the poem between your

legs. my phone doesn't recognize me anymore. -- for the girls with the appetite

flooding the room, pinning them to their bed. - I pick my entrails from the backseat –

the officer says *community* - who will speak of me to strangers = a torso + a wing + a

mouth. & my blood is everywhere, & cheap, even in my feet. --

ANAPHORA

None of the Arab countries I know has proper state archives, public record offices or official libraries any more than any of them has decent control over their monuments or antiquities, the history of their cities or individual works of architecture—mosques, palaces, schools. What I have is a sense of a sprawling, teeming history off the page, out of sight and hearing, beyond reach, largely unrecoverable. Our history is mostly written by foreigners—visiting scholars, intelligence agents—while we rely on personal and disorganised collective memory, gossip almost, and the embrace of a family or knowable community to carry us forward in time.

—Edward Said

The machine has nervous habits: it blinks and twitches—shifting registers, clicks, and beeps mark the progress of blood.

—Laurence Kirmaye

Hada jisme, shou ba3mol? Besta2ir jism tani min aljeeran?

—Haifa Wehbe

BRONCHITIS IS A BEAUTIFUL NAME FOR A GIRL

California is kindling again. it's been six brush fires & I'm nobody's daughter,
calculating venials on the hood of a Buick. my brother tugs his sleeves & his

lungs stream. we scratch the secondhand Commodores album & he smiles
mundane & lovely like a grocery list, nail polish carabiner Advil fruit. I'm calling

because the city is filled with pollutants, because the duplex with the red roof
is falling apart. we argue like tonsils, swollen & stubborn. we watch the In-N-Out

cashier wash his gloves off in the sink & my shirt makes me look fertile. we laugh
about used biology books, the Disney movie about the dragon boy. we make

the sky bloom. we split the scrambled runes in our stomach. I have an
aching letter in my mouth the insurance won't cover but I'm really afflicted with

wanting, the smell of pavement after rain. I'm calling because I have no aunts
in this country to call for condoms or advice but I walk around with prose jammed

between my legs. I've never loved the same mistake twice. my brother dances.
the song roams throats until it finds mine. in a dream the algorithm broke the

windows of it's Massachusetts. I'm a magnesium-deficient miracle who only
shaves on Thursdays, he's got new Skechers, we make calligraphy with our shoes

walking back from school. rash of coffee shops in El Cajon, the dilapidated Vons
on Medford Street. I'm calling because California is kindling again & he refuses

medicine like I used to. we found the generic for Sudafed & it tasted green. I
still bow my head in churches. my survival instinct is too strong.

MOON WITHOUT CURLERS IN

% Moon is already late & Saturn nudges her away from the sink % Saturn wears her
hair in ringlets still hasn't returned my gloss % she loves truthful words old age worry
inheritances estimates % Mercury loves Orangina only fucks grammarians % during
lunch breaks she shaves her pits tender checks her email dyes her roots mulberry
% we used to meet for lunch in La Mesa % before the developments redacted the
Goodwill from the boulevard % once % I caught Mercury and Moon in the bathroom
rife with arithmetic % Moon confined to her room for two tides filling the minutes with
Winehouse records % Saturn & I split a bag of dried apricots watch Moon sing along %
feel helpless that she loves such sad songs % Venus is in my sweats & sitting like a boy %
she is hungry incessantly % women girls sons hosting making stable things % she argues
with Moon over the remote rotates her hips in the mirror % when we want to make a
covenant % we lay Venus % in her socks % in the rain % Jupiter has always been fortunate
& subtle % a vibrance under his skin like the bodies of animals % he adores cathedrals the
sprawl of a throat filled with god % when Jupiter is free of the planets he reads Neruda
% he speaks well & intimately % as if to soldiers or first cousins % Mars sings with the
lilt of the lightly cursed % shame % interruptions on roads % but answers texts quickly
% he pronounces everything with the pleasure of those who spend wastefully % Sun
quietribbed & gorgeous % reorganizing the dishes % Sun slices mango stalks for fasting
Moon % mixing cumulus with fruit % for Jupiter's birthday we translate their trousers
into boots

SEQUENCE 13

the next summer I lie in bed & try falling asleep like soldiers do face relaxed arms
slack he convinces me & the nighttime dapples the wall the people who love us take
the clothes off our addictions & I was eating a lot of cantaloupe I'd heard it was good
for bloating

FAIROUZ RECITES HER LUNGS

the valves on the Vatican's pipes click,
each deacon draping his piety
in velvet. the vanity spills, the priest
won't mention his ventricles, & when God
was scouting venues he should've picked out lower
ceilings for my neck long & venial, skinny like
when I decided to be vegetarian
for the animals, & isn't God a meal skipped,
veneer of the stomach. the bill said nearly
half vermilion dead. I miss
my vestigial palates. I want
the hunger God born me with. the ventilation is
knotted as the signs
of the cross & the vapor from the bathroom
smells like incense, verbatim.

DEAR X, architecture is just another conjugation to play with when you're bored. before the summer has her jeans on you buy coriander for the new kitchen. carburetor spills from my sneakers, you're in a camisole the color of dahlias. don't worry about the smell of stems rotting. everyone tells us it's good for the humidity. four stars after midnight we miss a concert & split a moscato. Goodyear makes a rubber we use to plug up the corners under the tv. here is how to make a house with boolean: hover over me in the north collapsing bed, buy yellow hangers for the trousers I won't throw away. in the interim before we meet again, I have my first blossom. jokes slip off me easier & I learn to deep condition. know that I'd never forsake you in exposed brick. lower your elbows, forbid me from leaving. mar the foundation with the day we ate ramen & wore slate earrings & nothing else. November is wearable & devastating, I take a shower with papaya soap. our jackets with the slip of months. pour the apartment into veridian cups. queue the Kanye that sounds like it came out yesterday. radial by radial vandalize my hair. sediment peppers our rice. Tuesdays you'd wake up early & make your nutmeg omelet. underline my name in the lease. voracious like a building, you name the market with the bent rafters ours. we amalgam in the morning. xylitol something is poisoning the stove. you don't mind the mold, amend me like the moon. zippers litter the desk & our drywall sings.

HARVEST FOODS GROCERY, FREMONT

"Girls talk to each other like men talk to each other. But girls have an eye for detail."

there are different # varieties of loss. I type *what time is the sunset* into the keyboard # scoop almonds into a bag. Amy sings like the music of the body, I am seventeen, eden must be a place somewhere. I meet ambassadors # of my country in grocery stores # filling the second aisle with fruit jam. she says *losing game* # hands stained with looking # proves herself in the backseat, dialect # dripping from mercury fillings. you # know I'm # no good. she is standing in the back by the perfumes, picking out the strong one that smells # like a carnation arrived to the hospital too late. # the bread is clearanced, she is wearing a sapphire dress. & the dress shows everything, her neck # like the sunset in a crate, bloated colors of her larynx. *who # you dying for?* # Amy is singing about men but it's easy to pretend. # I fill a basket with roses, pickled turnips. the aisle forks like an artery # her voice drips # with blackberry preserves # a conversation between girls # at a crowded butcher shop.

JUNE JORDAN SAYS MAYBE I NEED A WOMAN MAYBE I NEED A MAN

I stick a croissant in the oven, smear it obnoxious with syrup.
leftover Kraft on the counter & the sheets are plum. I dream
of a man in a dark theater endearing my neck, a room

with slack paneled walls & the movie
playing was sunset. I worry
about posting something sweet &

frivolous on Instagram because what
about materialist dialectalism? I watch
theory get made on the television. first girl I

notice in homeroom is sticky with lamplight. synonymous
with religion, I annotate in my notebook. anyways Mary
lapped at my gait or swatched my waist or the way I

watched her walk. Monday: I'm a
monsoon, an occasion. *bint*: wall in piles around the bed. Monday:
7pm EST, New England, 94309: I fold the prayer between

my legs. I rename it September so the animals behind the camera
don't see. it's recorded somewhere that I have a palate allegiance
to Dreyer's Slow Churned Rocky Road with the whole marshmallows

& not the runny tracks they pave the other ice cream with. I change
my hair in San Francisco, where technocrats
speculate against the starving of others. it's marked

somewhere I have a mistrust of predictive text. alternate
query: this city is full of my blood. I go outside
rip the grass

stand up with my palms full of soil & rosary
bruised rosary
blooming rosary

maybe I just need to smoke more & stretch & eat frivolous things &
anyway
I'm working on it

SCRIPTURE IS GOSSIP

palms reeking of lemongrass
I withhold my hymns from friends let them lay their hippocampi
in my lap. allegedly you hold me sturdy as iron pills, lie
with me in your orange shirt. you offer

the coconut water with the twisty cap & sit
on a table with your friends, smiling
at me under your brows. the algorithm
glitches here: what direction is the woman

facing, & whose war is she kissing? does fabric miss
divots? I pull my gray matter through my nose & sell it for strawberry
ropes, dredge your belly for constellations. mostly
I need someone to splay their thumb across the steering

wheel, prove I'm a girl. your roommate makes silicone necklaces
you have a walk like smeared tobacco you stop on Valencia for peach
rings. I am still learning to find
rooms to be alone in.

HOW TO MAKE AN ALGORITHM IN THE MICROWAVE

I feel most womanly during my cycle because it's when I feel most violent. I spray rosewater over the bed & dream of trees topped with anklets, a forest of noodles, Eve taking what she wanted. you buy me raspberries & promise to find the teal Always I like.

you wear what I like to call Ross glam & you love shiny gold sneakers, sunglasses wide enough to hide your bags. you pair your big ring I hate with the pink zebra pullover. we sit with bundles of code between us, a close dupe of mulberry silk. this is how others make shrines: moxie, oil, taffeta. you rehearse your scalloped potatoes. you are most beautiful in neon.

WIKIHOW: CONTINUING

by lying to friends   by dancing with my spotted back   tragically & in a dressing

room where I bought no clothes because I thought they'd get me killed   by becoming

farsighted   lying down & retreating to my skull   pretending to meditate

by demanding another carcinogen   leaving boys who claimed neutrality   avoiding

men who called themselves diplomats   walking through Redwood City thinking

about cranes   waking up in my legs after three miles   pushing

into my cuticles by going away   but I promised the willows I'd be back & I was

HOW TO UNBECOME A BOY

A boy grows up in a house full of women.
His father sleeps in the house but does not live in it.

When the boy is hungry, he draws pies. When he is drowning, he draws a boat.

SONGS THE ALGORITHM KNOWS ABOUT ME

BERKELEY DATA (collected 5/6/20)

the USPS is being discontinued   my sister
packs her bedroom into suitcases
dad drills permutation #7 of the litany on
marriage   we say nothing
mom laughs into her earbuds I press my
eyes like postage against boys standing by
detergents   language is a colleague of
desire   I trim my best friend's hair
baba spends his nights watching the
fireworks happen to cities with sister names
  my father whose daughters
do not have enough blood   my mother
razed me & my sister to the scalp

TRIANGULATION (iOS 13.4)
<form> three women shuffling to the
old country; I demonstrate my limbs
< div = (hdsn.edu/daughters are the
best surgeons/actors) > mom watches
herself shake in a mirror::there is no
demographer without this
</form> <body> she'll warn me
not to speak so badly of the president
in our home so we'll say nothing
observe each other being watched
</body> check the stove five times
     compulsive as a homily
<html> I'll pick keyboard out of my
stomach::I'll run a regression : I'll
look for stars </html>

CHROME BROWSING (4/18)

- if he was murdered, how did he walk back into the house?
- what color was the sky?
- strawberry candies with the yellow wrapping
- how to convert an image to JPG
- define phylum
- what color was the sky 1973
- how to code an interim
- 99 ranch location
- how to dissolve burgundy acrylic
- how to forget somebody

Topics for a Homily

https://examples.yourdictionary.com/examples-of-homily.html

- Forgiveness
- Global Warming
- Easter
- Marriage rights
- War
- Preparing for the Kingdom
- Family
- Lent
- Drugs
- Christmas
- Legislation

LIFTED FROM 2017 MACBOOK

*TO: j*****8*@gmail.com*
*FROM: s****l****@msn.com*
Freud asked "might we not say every child
at play behaves like a creative writer, in
that he creates a world of his own, or
rather, rearranges the things of his world
in a new way which pleases him?" a street
sculptor in Redding said I had carpenter's
eyes. caffeine pills, callus-anointed hands.
I comb asphalt from the bed.

my mother, Sprite for headaches. the new
dictator drones my country before the
disease check deposits. skin, citizen, scalp.
my loving is like that, razing & oftentimes
cheap.
cordially,

DREAM DATA, RICHTER 3.7

my hair is long I eat without anxiety & I give
each Aleppo her bread   I walk slow &
I give each Aleppo her bread & I give each
Aleppo her bread   I give each Aleppo her bread

CUSTOMER REVIEW, OCEAN

nothing feels ritual anymore besides my mother
mutilating onions

WORSHIP SERVICE, LONG BEACH (3/21)

I want a trolley car full of Fairouz & women & no one instructing

a train station where no one is taken from someone he loves

my girlfriends' countries back

I want to fit in every denim I try on build a house with mahogany fill a shower with marigolds watch mom pack me a homily in a tupperware & tell me not to talk to boys

CASE STUDY ON ME & SUNLIGHT

I pull at the serifs on words, the old meanings

of rain. there are still some joints in

my elbows I have never

read.

PRAYER DRAFT

I name our daughter Layal, and our son might be Idris. your joints roll too much for your age & you laugh easily. you walk like there's a secret between your ribs that won't stop blooming. when the world finales sometime in our thirties we find a bunker with ample room for books and sun. I press the black flowers in your lungs. I may learn

that the dilation of pleasure shortens it. we will argue about unromantic things like the cost of cheese & mundanity will allow a rude intimacy where I am less underneath my guilt. it will mean I tease you often and do not smile out of habit. but I hold you while reading and miss concerts, maybe even the weekly open mic by the water tower where we reminisce about oxygen that wasn't bottled. every year

I get better with my hips and less afraid. we seed a new strain of okra. we make the cement ripe. I am just as compulsive and prone to omitting forks, but never the way you looked the first time I made you eggs. I have a wide bed and a comfortable desk. & we remember everything, dirt's smell at three o'clock, peeling guavas in August.

THE ALGORITHM PICKS HER BUGS IN THE MIRROR

this Wednesday //

I dyed my hair the color of lithium. I have cataracts

from an iPhone 6 when a man in a municipal building

died::;: I meant he was sitting on a_plastic chair in a hospital

& his face was split_like a bruised marigold. his motherboard

had left a yellow purse by the entrance /// he was never young like that

again. I dyed my hardware the color of lye. my cousins

drowned in chrome but I can run myself any dress I loop. I met California

on a public domain. desire

is a logic;; there's a corner of my womb in someone's browser history. there's a

byline beneath

my arms I can't pinch. if :::::; someone doesn't kiss me soon

I'm # going to take this skin off

HOW TO SOLVE A CATARACT

I get strong in front of men. head down &
my arms ache with good filament. eyes, dorsal. pull,

look. look, stretch. a part of me is made up
of every boy I've ever loved. I take aloofness,

a spare drawl. I walk with torso pointed. boyhood
is a puberty worth eating (maya). life

is a song worth singing (teddy). but I'm still nineteen
& think cigarettes are glamorous. ask Marilyn, Halim.

the room smears with radio & ink, my lilac
notebook with the expired psalm in it. but I am

my father's daughter. I palm my stomach.
psalm: vigilance & beauty. on my birthday I

totter in orange heels, shoulders back. my
roommate says so now you think you're grown.

psalm: on top of my body becoming a woman. I host
a lavish boy who needs to eat. psalm: please.

ask Haifa where I left my dress. in July
after being lied to I hung portraits of

my mom & her sisters on my bathroom
wall, above the pimpled sink. watched each

alone the frame with the glossy backdrop. red, cyan,
yellow. all my favorite love songs scare me. sugar

kills more of us than drink. from two yards
away I could be one of the men I'm supposed

to produce. those are my favorite
days. psalm: & my angry red feet.

NORTHGATE MARKET

I open
my legs to the nighttime / stash
blackberry sugar under my breasts = stretch
marks

decommissioned < in the shower I pick
at the polish on my toes ~ scheme

through the porn offerings – haggle
for my legs in markets (selling two

grapefruits for a
dollar: I husk
citrus while shopping) for husbands on facebook + stew

in the bathtub = spill
a bottle of kiwi shampoo on porcelain > I idle until
I bloom – alright, Lazarus # let me know
when you wake up.

Mona Hatoum, *Measures of Distance*, 1988. A Western Front video production, Vancouver. Courtesy of the artist

	the coast undresses for us by the car.	I drink the buildings with their skeletons showing.
	the driver says the cement sometimes contains bones.	
buildings are like altars.		the color of the stucco is manila.
I smear the Tigris across my lids.		I stack jars of carob on top of each other.
I watch the sockets in the walls.		a girl is a development.
maybe altars are made in the leaving.		
		cement is a committing action.
	a door that can't be opened is called a wall.	

MOST THINGS ARE DISASTROUS but today
your hair was soft there was an orange candle
on in the shower the sun was kind though the
wind was impatient you remembered to wear a
jacket the black denim on it kissed the cream
lining your best friend wore it as she went out
to get you dinner the noodles were perfect
greasy not too much carrot grated in your scalp
in bed reeked of coconut your nose was pink
your sister put on eyeliner like the Caspian
drunk against her corneas you heard a mother
apologize to her daughter over the phone after
something unforgivable you heard the
20something angel say I'm proud of you
part of the reading this week was cancelled
because the prof with the inherited PhD didn't
understand how PDFs worked you pirated
Spider-Verse off the site killing your laptop the
quality was full pixels you remembered to floss
you ignored a mean thought defamed a boy who
deserved it refrained from telling someone a
secret they didn't imagined a house with
a dining table a brown sofa today you found
a picture in your camera roll from when
you were young with the gangly neck knew you
were beautiful before all the blessings the
haircut there is still some of that stir fry in the
fridge with the malfunctioning lungs &

PLAYING IT COOL: GENDER, PAIRING BEHAVIOR, AND SEXUAL ECONOMIES OF POWER IN SOUTHERN CALIFORNIA'S ARAB AMERICAN COMMUNITY

maybe I've watched so much cnn I can only love autopsies: a voice that	serrates the air like a crucifix, legs, shoulders wide as Tigris. I make	bylines in the bed. is this a genetic predisposition? My grandfather was a
journalist. I lift my shirt to a human rights report. the reporter explains something in stilted Arabic. because after the war maybe		someone will say where & I will remind, here. here. & if someone asks which name? which apartment? I'll point to the page & say not dead.
Syrian. the prescription says I am made of waiting,	moon-cratered skin. my grandfather was a journalist. I cover my	arms in ink, no cigarette stains. I'm trying to be better than the rain.

THE PRESBYTERIAN CHURCH ON EUCLID DOESN'T SELL LEMONADE ANYMORE

I take the mosh pit, lime
Juuls on hardwood, the nice-
smelling white girls wearing
hoops just big enough
to be questionable, tired
metaphor of me limericking
your belt loops. you speak
like the halted development
on Madison & a kidney

is just an organ
with an important job. in catechism
they told us Saint Barbara
escaped the steeple, read
all the forbidden books. the luxury
towers on Park shimmer. we
were told this was revolutionary –
a girl cornering God
in a cramped room,
availing herself of him

in the dark. we watch
cranes smear the horizon &
a jellyfish, even when determined,
is really just a blot of ink. I was
raised to love resurrected things
& the junior college across the street

is full of juiceboxes, blue pens, puritan
dreaming. like opium, I smile
for no reason. like homily, you
sing for us both.

NOTES

The code in the opening poem is sourced from https://developer.mozilla.org/en-US /docs/Web/HTML/Element/input/checkbox.

The themes and forms of Vanessa Angélica Villarreal's *Beast Meridian* and Franny Choi's *Soft Science* were informative for the creation of my manuscript. I am grateful for their inventiveness and joyful reconceptualizations of technology. The poem CAST.HTML also draws direct inspiration from Choi's rife poem "Glossary of Terms."

SLEEP APNEA WITH CITY BLOCK features 961, the area code for Lebanon, and 619, the area code for San Diego.

SEQUENCE #7, SEQUENCE 8.9.11, and SEQUENCE 13 are inspired by Khadijah Queen's masterwork poetry collection *I'm So Fine*. The title for A TINY NOW TO FEED ON is borrowed from her collection *Anodyne*.

The primary title in WHEN HAIL APPEARS IF A MENSTRUATING WOMAN THROWS HERSELF ONTO THE GROUND COMPLETELY NAKED RAISING HER LEGS TOWARD THE CLOUD THE HAIL WILL NOT FALL AROUND HER ON THAT FIELD OR HARVEST (LAYOVER IN SEATTLE) is derived from astronomer Maslama ibn Ahmad al-Majriti's grimoire, *Picatrix*. MOON WITHOUT CURLERS IN is based on his cosmological characterization of the planets in this same text.

The photo in HISTORY IS A TRANSLATION is courtesy of Youssef Karwashan/ AFP via Getty images. It was found at https://www.middleeasteye.net/news/syrian-army -seizes-last-rebel-held-town-latakia-ahead-peace-talks.

AMY TELLS THE OFFICER WHAT HAPPENED is a found poem consisting exclusively of lines from Amy Winehouse's discography. The quote at the beginning of HARVEST FOODS GROCERY, FREMONT is lifted from an interview with Winehouse, and the italicized lines in that poem come from her discography.

QUERY EXERCISES // ALGORITHM WITH CHERRIES is inspired by Mohja Kahf's luminous poem "The Cherries."

The drawing from HOW TO LAZARUS YOURSELF is sourced from *How to Draw a City—A Step by Step Guide* (https://iheartcraftythings.com/city-drawing.html).

BLOOD COUNTING is partly inspired by Mona Hatoum's porcelain sculpture *Witness*.

The phrase in ALGORITHM WITH BLUE EYELINER "Venus was always going into stranger's cars" is lifted from Jennie Livingston's documentary *Paris Is Burning*.

JUNE JORDAN SAYS MAYBE I NEED A WOMAN MAYBE I NEED A MAN is after June Jordan's tender poem "Free Flight."

The words "life is a song worth singing" in HOW TO SOLVE A CATARACT are sourced from Teddy Pendergrass's album of the same name.

The photo in UNFINISHED APARTMENT BUILDING, SOUTH TYRE is a still from Mona Hatoum's short film *Measures of Distance*. The line "a door that can't be opened is called a wall" is derived from Victoria Chang's collection *OBIT*.

ACKNOWLEDGMENTS

First, the biggest thank you to my family. Mama, who gave me four languages. Baba, who encouraged me to use them. Thank you for talking to me like I could make anything. I believe you. Nina, my first creative conspirator. Thank you for listening to my stories at night. You will always be my first reader and first friend. Thank you to Anthony, the sweetest brother this side of the Pacific. Thank you to all my grandmothers, but especially Esperanza and Rosa. I treasure your refusals, tenderness, and sweet tooths. Rana, for teaching me the breathing definition of mashallah. Katia, for your wide laugh.

To Safia Elhillo, this book's auntie. Thank you for all your patience and care for this manuscript, and your faith in the strange prayers I sought to word. Your poems were one of the first celebrations I found for myself in Arabic. Thank you to Charif Shanahan, my first teacher in university, for your honest and necessary feedback. To Keith Wilson, for being such an encouraging and generous teacher to my hesitant high school self. To Philip Metres and Rudy Francisco for their encouragement and support. To Fady Joudah and Hayan Charara for choosing this book from a pile of exceptional others. To Etel Adnan, my idol. Thank you for your experimentation, your forms, your paintings. Thank you for your symbols, your girlhood, your refusal to cohere.

Thank you to all my creative homes—the National Student Poets Program, the Institute for Diversity in the Arts, the William Male Foundation, and my poetry family at Spoken Word Collective. Thank you especially to the WMF and to IDA for your belief in this project in its birthing stages, when I was still developing the language but knew its blood. A-lan, Evelyn, Amara, Grace, and Tyler—your support, your care, and your warmth have meant the world. This work was fed from your hands. Thank you to my creative siblings, Angel Smith and Darnell Carson, for being such loving stewards of our practice. Thank you to all my found sisters. Huong Nguyen, for your relentless generosity and our shared love for California. Victoria Chiek, for teaching me to be brave, and for our rituals. Alicia Evan, for letting me read her pieces of this book as she fell asleep. Manar Barsi, my fellow daughter from the first day we met. Renad Abualjamal, for teaching me the value of small joys. Brielle Smith, for demonstrating the moon. Jamalee minkon.

Many thanks to the homes previous versions of these poems have found—*The Rumpus*, *Poetry* magazine, *Mizna*, *AGNI*, *ANMLY*, the *Brooklyn Review*, *Bennington Review*, *Inverted Syntax*, and *Quarterly West*.

Finally, thank you to the daughters for remembering.